Original title:
Butterfly Barriers

Copyright © 2024 Creative Arts Management OÜ
All rights reserved.

Author: Theodore Sinclair
ISBN HARDBACK: 978-9916-90-582-1
ISBN PAPERBACK: 978-9916-90-583-8

Unseen Walls of Delicate Grace

Whispers dance in silent air,
Echoes weave a tender snare.
Shadows cling to fragile sights,
Hidden worlds in gentle flights.

Softly wrapped in secret dreams,
Veils of time in silver beams.
Truths concealed behind the hues,
Unseen walls where hearts enthuse.

Fluttering Beyond the Veil

Feathers fall in hushed delight,
Lifting hopes towards the light.
Moments drift like autumn leaves,
In stillness, the spirit believes.

Beyond the veil, a song unfolds,
Whispers echo, stories told.
Each flutter, a chance to see,
The beauty of what's meant to be.

Barriers Beneath the Spectrum

Colors merge and often blur,
Underneath, the heart's soft stir.
Barriers lie in shades unseen,
Veiling aspects of the serene.

Light refracts in subtle ways,
Chasing shadows, weaving rays.
Beneath the surface, bonds can break,
Yet from their shards, new paths we make.

Translucent Journeys in Stillness

A journey starts without a sound,
In the stillness, peace is found.
Translucent paths where spirits roam,
In quietude, we find our home.

Footsteps trace the unseen road,
Upon the heart, a heavy load.
Yet every step, though slow it seems,
Leads us closer to our dreams.

The Silent Song of Unraveled Flight

In twilight's hush, the shadows play,
Soft echoes swirl, then drift away.
A heart once bold, now bound to earth,
Yearns for the sky, for rebirth's worth.

Beneath the stars, a flicker gleams,
Dreams tethered tight to whispered dreams.
A melody lost in gentle sighs,
The silent song where hope still lies.

Fluttering Whispers Against the Grain

A breeze strokes feathers with gentle care,
Whispers dart and dance; they fill the air.
Against the tide, they twist and bend,
In every flutter, a message they send.

Through tangled woods, beneath the sun,
Songs of the brave, their journey begun.
With every beat, defiance sings,
Fluttering whispers on daring wings.

Wings Caught in a Web

Threads of silver, tightly spun,
A heart ensnared, where dreams are none.
In silence trapped, a prayer takes flight,
Wings caught at dusk, in fading light.

The struggle soft, yet fierce the fight,
Against the pull of the web's delight.
In every snare, a strength revealed,
A spirit fierce, a fate unsealed.

The Flight That Dared Not Soar

A timid heart on tender wings,
Held back by doubts, the silence stings.
Beneath the clouds, the shadows loom,
A whispered wish, a heart's quiet gloom.

Yet dreams still flicker, deep within,
A spark that dares to rise and spin.
With courage born from shadow's lore,
A promise waits, to brave the floor.

Whispers That Carry

In the hush of twilight's glow,
Soft secrets linger, ebb and flow.
Voices merge with starry night,
Echoes dance, a fleeting flight.

Gentle winds weave tender tales,
Carried far on silver trails.
In the dark, they intertwine,
Whispers call, forever mine.

Coiled Dreams of the Wandering Heart

In the shadows, dreams awake,
Wandering souls, their paths they take.
With every twist, hope intertwines,
Coiled within the heart's confines.

A journey vast, with stars to chase,
Each heartbeat finds its hidden place.
Through valleys deep and mountains high,
Dreams may wander, they won't die.

Breaths Caught in Still Air

Silent moments, breaths stand still,
Nature's pulse, soft and shrill.
Underneath the weight of time,
Whispers linger, a gentle chime.

Eyes closed tight, we feel the breath,
Life suspended, dancing with death.
In stillness, secrets come alive,
Caught in time, we learn to thrive.

The Beauty of Unattainable Sky

Beyond the reach of weary hands,
Lies a sky where freedom stands.
Painted hues of dreams untold,
A canvas rich, a sight to behold.

The clouds may tease with silver linings,
Yet the height holds endless findings.
In the gaze, our hearts may soar,
Chasing whispers of evermore.

Songs of Silent Transformation

In shadows deep, a whisper flows,
The silent heart, in stillness grows.
A dance of change, unseen yet bright,
Emerging strong, from darkest night.

Each breath a step, new paths unveil,
Through hidden doors, we start to sail.
Transformation sings, in muted tones,
A brave rebirth, from quiet stones.

Soft Whispers Between Bars

In narrow halls, where shadows play,
The softest words have much to say.
Between the bars, a truth unspun,
A gentle hope, like morning sun.

With every breath, a secret shared,
In silent bonds, we are ensnared.
The weight of walls, a fleeting sigh,
In whispers soft, our spirits fly.

Freedom in Moonlit Heartbeats

Beneath the glow of silver light,
Our hearts awaken, taking flight.
In every beat, a promise true,
The night reveals what dreams imbue.

With every pulse, the chains release,
A dance of joy, a rush of peace.
In moonlit realms, we find our way,
A symphony of night and day.

Tides of Color

Colors clash in wild embrace,
A canvas drawn with vibrant grace.
Tides that swell and ebb with time,
In hues that dance, a secret rhyme.

From azure skies to crimson shores,
Life's palette flows, forever pours.
In every shade, a story told,
A spectrum bright, a heart of gold.

Prices of Flight

To soar above, the cost is steep,
Yet dreams unwind, in silence creep.
Each feather lost, a tale of gain,
As freedom's call, ignites the pain.

In trials faced, we learn to rise,
With every fall, we touch the skies.
The prices paid for wings of light,
Are worth the journey, in the night.

Gossamer Dreams Unraveled

In twilight's soft embrace, they fade,
Fragile threads of hopes once made.
Whispers lost in evening's sigh,
Gossamer dreams that fluttered high.

Amidst the stars, with hearts in flight,
We chased the moon, elusive light.
Yet shadows creep, the night descends,
A tapestry undone, it ends.

What once was bright now drapes in gray,
The dreams we spun begin to fray.
In silence, echoes start to blend,
Unraveled hopes, they break and bend.

Silent Wings

A hush falls soft on whispered air,
Silent wings tread without a care.
They glide through realms of dimming light,
Carrying secrets out of sight.

With every flap, a tale unfolds,
Of silent journeys and stories told.
They brush the night with feathered grace,
In twilight's arms, they find their place.

Yet shadows linger, dark and deep,
Where weary hearts and sorrows seep.
These silent wings, though smooth and grand,
Bear quiet burdens we understand.

Shattered Paths

A road once clear, now lost in grey,
Shattered dreams lead hearts astray.
Footsteps echo where none should be,
In tangled weeds, we seek to see.

With every turn, a memory shines,
Each broken piece, a hint of lines.
Lost in the labyrinth of our fears,
We tread with echoes of silent tears.

Fragments glisten, yet cut so deep,
Promises made, we strive to keep.
Yet on this path where shadows loom,
Hope blossoms softly, dispelling gloom.

The Colors of a Prison

Behind the bars, a canvas bright,
Brush strokes of sorrow mixed with light.
Colors bleed where shadows blend,
The prison walls begin to bend.

Each hue holds tales of dreams confined,
Of hearts once bold, now undefined.
Yet in this space, a spark ignites,
The colors dance with daring flights.

What seems to bind can also free,
A palette rich with possibility.
In every shade, we find our voice,
In muted tones, we still rejoice.

Embracing the Unseen Chains

Invisible chains, they pull so tight,
Binding our souls in the shrouded night.
Yet in the struggle, strength we find,
Embracing bonds that once confined.

Each link a lesson, forged in fire,
Steering our hearts, stoking desire.
Though unseen chains may weigh us down,
They craft the paths on which we frown.

With open arms, we greet the fight,
For through the dark, we seek the light.
In every struggle, growth remains,
Embracing life, despite the chains.

Fractured Flight

Beneath the weight of shattered dreams,
A sky that whispers lost extremes.
The broken wings of silent cries,
In every gust, the spirit sighs.

The echoes of a fading might,
In shadows cast by waning light.
Each feather torn, a memory,
A tale of what was meant to be.

In winds that brush the jagged edge,
A heart ensnared in fate's own ledge.
Yet still, the whispers urge me on,
To find a way 'ere hope is gone.

Through fractured dreams, I'll take to air,
And dance with spirits unaware.
With every rise and every fall,
I'll write my story through it all.

The Ink of Broken Wings

Upon the page, the sorrow spills,
Inky trails of lingering ills.
A feathered quill, once strong and bold,
Now writes the tales of dreams turned cold.

The ink flows deep, a river wide,
Of heartache kept and tears that bide.
With every stroke, the truth unfolds,
Of loving hearts and stories told.

Yet even broken, wings can rise,
To chase the sun in painted skies.
In every drop of darkened lore,
A hint of light behind that door.

So let the ink, though tarnished, flow,
To weave the stories we all know.
For in this dance of pain and art,
The ink of broken wings finds heart.

Chasing Light Through Mist

In early dawn, the world awakes,
Through tendrils of the mist that shakes.
With every step, the shadows play,
As light begins to greet the day.

I wander through the hazy veil,
Where whispers weave a ghostly tale.
Each flicker bright, a fleeting chance,
To break the spell and dream a dance.

The sun breaks free, a golden thread,
Igniting paths where few have tread.
In every ray, a promise glows,
To chase that light where passion flows.

So here I stand, amidst the mist,
With every beat, the shadows twist.
To chase the light, untangle night,
And find my way 'neath skies so bright.

Barriers of Petal and Pain

In gardens deep, where silence reigns,
The petals bloom through layers of pain.
Each fragrance rich, a story told,
Of beauty found in struggles bold.

Yet thorns that pierce in soft embrace,
Remind me of the bitter chase.
To reach for joy, I tread the line,
Between the hurt and love divine.

The colors dance in gentle sway,
A tapestry of night and day.
With every tear, the petals gleam,
Like whispered hopes, they light the dream.

So let me walk this narrow path,
Embrace the joy, endure the wrath.
In barriers, both pain and grace,
I find my truth, I find my place.

Dreams That Wear Chains

In shadows deep, where whispers cling,
Hopes are bound with iron rings.
Each desire screams to break away,
Yet silence holds the light of day.

In corners dim, the visions fade,
A tapestry of dreams betrayed.
The heart beats loud against the night,
Yearning for a chance to fight.

With every sigh, a breath of fear,
The chains they rattle, always near.
But deep within, a spark ignites,
To spark a path through the endless fights.

So let the dreams, though chained, still soar,
For boundless skies await once more.
In every heart, the hope remains,
To rise beyond these heavy chains.

Fluttering within Walls

Inside these walls, the echoes dance,
A butterfly caught, lost in a trance.
Fluttering wings, a gentle plea,
Craving the world beyond what we see.

The windows close, the shadows crawl,
Yet whispers of freedom still enthrall.
With every flap, a chance to break,
To trace the skies, the air to take.

But fears confine, like heavy stone,
Yet hope persists, though all alone.
With every twirl, a light does gleam,
The urge to chase a wild dream.

So flutter on, sweet soul of grace,
Leap beyond this sheltered space.
For even walls can't keep the heart,
From seeking out its destined start.

The Sigh of a Flickering Flame

A candle burns, the shadows sway,
The flicker dances, night and day.
With every breath, the flame will sigh,
A whispered wish into the sky.

The warmth it shares, a tender glow,
In darkest hours, it seeks to show.
The fragile light, it trembles still,
Yet holds the power of gentle will.

In every flicker, stories live,
Embers tale what time can give.
A moment brief, yet deeply felt,
Through every breath, the heartbeat melts.

As long as fire lights the night,
Its silence speaks, a language right.
For in that sigh, a soul's embrace,
The flicker knows its cherished place.

Prism of Imprisoned Wishes

In every corner, dreams are trapped,
A prism bright, where hopes are wrapped.
Each colorful sigh, a silent plea,
Reflects the light of what could be.

With jagged edges, the glass remains,
Holding tightly to fractured chains.
Yet through the cracks, the colors spill,
Painting shadows on the hill.

In every hue, a story weaves,
Echoes of what the heart believes.
Imprisoned wishes, bright and bold,
Waiting for the hand to hold.

So let the light shine through the bars,
Transforming pain into bright stars.
For in this prism, life shall dance,
A symphony of lost romance.

Reflections on Fragile Wings

In the quiet night, they soar high,
Soft whispers of dreams, as they fly.
Delicate frames, a dance in the breeze,
Holding the pulse of the world with ease.

Mirrors of twilight on silken air,
Glimmers of hope, bright and rare.
Yet shadows linger, a haunting refrain,
The fragility woven in joy and pain.

They flicker like stars in the vast unknown,
Carrying tales of places they've flown.
Each beat of their hearts, a story unfolds,
Of fleeting moments that memory holds.

With every rise, there comes a fall,
A lesson of depth, a gentle call.
On fragile wings, in the still of the night,
We find our solace, we find our light.

Ensnared in a Tangle of Beauty

Petals entwined in the softest embrace,
Colors collide in a vibrant space.
Nature's allure, a spell it weaves,
In tangled rhythms, the heart believes.

Whispers of jasmine and sweet summer rain,
Each fragrance a memory, joy, and pain.
The tapestry woven, both bold and shy,
In a world of beauty, we learn to fly.

Amidst the thorns, a rose does bloom,
In every shadow, there's light to consume.
Caught in the dance of the season's song,
In a tangle of beauty, we find where we belong.

But beware the charm that draws us in tight,
For in every dream, there hides a slight fright.
In the maze of allure, we tread with care,
Embracing the beauty, aware of the snare.

Colors Lost in the Fog

In the morning mist, the colors fade,
A watercolor world, softly laid.
Shapes disappear in the silent haze,
Lost in the depths of memory's maze.

Once vibrant hues, now shades of grey,
Whispers of life in disarray.
Fields once golden, now muted and cold,
Stories untold in the fog enfold.

Yet in the gloom, a glimmer remains,
A spark of warmth that life sustains.
Embers of colors, fighting to break,
Through layers of fog, they choose to awake.

In the shroud, we search for the light,
Guided by hope, dispelling the night.
For even in shadows, the colors can gleam,
Awakening dreams we once thought just a dream.

The Weight of Fleeting Freedom

Beneath the sky, the heart takes flight,
In search of horizons, a new insight.
Chains of the past, we long to break,
Chasing the dawn, for freedom's sake.

But freedom whispers a delicate tale,
A weight we carry, a binding sail.
For every choice, a consequence hidden,
In the game of life, we are often bidden.

Soaring high, yet tethered below,
Reveling in winds, while we learn to grow.
The cost of the chase, the thrill of the race,
In the arms of freedom, we find our place.

Yet as we dance on the edges of time,
The fleeting moments turn into rhyme.
In the weight of freedom, we learn to be,
A journey of hearts, forever set free.

Metamorphosis of the Heart

In shadows deep, the heart does yearn,
For whispers soft, for flames that burn.
A fragile bud begins to bloom,
Transforming sorrow into room.

With courage found, the chains unbind,
New colors rise, a love refined.
From ashes cold, a fire starts,
Awakening the hidden parts.

Seasons change, the heart grows wise,
With every tear, a new sunrise.
Embracing pain, the beauty grows,
In every wound, a story flows.

With time, the heart learns to forgive,
In letting go, we learn to live.
A dance of souls, a sacred spark,
In metamorphosis, we embark.

Whispers of the Restrained Wings

Beneath the clouds, the silence dwells,
A world of dreams where longing swells.
The wings of fate, they stretch and plead,
In gentle whispers, a heart's true need.

Each feathered hope, a tale to tell,
Of skies unseen and breaking shells.
A chorus soft, the muted cries,
In every heart, a chance to rise.

The tethered flight, yet spirits soar,
In daring hearts, there lies much more.
Restrained but yearning, they seek the skies,
To dance with stars and claim their prize.

In fleeting moments, courage blooms,
As freedom calls amid the glooms.
With eyes wide open, they pave the way,
For whispered dreams that dare to stay.

Liquid Light and Stolen Moments

In twilight's glow, the world unwinds,
As liquid light in stillness binds.
A fleeting glance, a crash of waves,
In stolen moments, the heart behaves.

Golden hues, the dusk's embrace,
Each second etched, a sacred space.
With whispered breaths, the night adheres,
To tender joys and unshed tears.

The dance of time, so sweetly spun,
Captures laughter, whispers fun.
Every heartbeat, a sigh of grace,
In the tapestry of time and space.

In liquid light, the shadows play,
As stolen moments fade away.
Yet in their wake, the memories gleam,
A treasure trove, a fleeting dream.

The Tapestry of Transience

Threads of gold weave through the night,
In every stitch, a soft ignite.
The fabric bends, the colors blend,
In transient beauty, we find our mend.

With every breath, a fleeting chance,
In moments crafted, we take a dance.
A fleeting touch, a gaze, a sigh,
The tapestry whispers, time slips by.

Embrace the flow, let go of chains,
In every loss, a new gains.
Life's woven stories, bright and pale,
A tapestry rich, a fragile tale.

In twilight's glow, we trace our paths,
With love and laughter, through all the laughs.
For transient moments, we hold dear,
In life's mosaic, forever near.

Delicate Struggles of Flight

Wings unfurl in heavy air,
A tug of gravity's grip.
Birds of dreams begin to dare,
With every rise, they slowly slip.

Currents shift, a whispered plea,
Beneath the weight of silent skies.
Softly, they beg to be free,
Yet the ground calls with heavy sighs.

Each flap tells a tale of hope,
Navigating doubts that bind.
Through storms, they learn to cope,
Finding strength in the undefined.

In the end, they take to flight,
Painting arcs in brightened hue.
Delicate struggles give them sight,
For freedom's gift is something new.

A Dance Behind Glass

Figures sway in a muted glow,
Shadows twist in gentle light.
Each movement speaks, yet none can know,
The sorrows hiding from their sight.

Reflections spin on surface clear,
Waltzing dreams that come and go.
Silent laughter hides a tear,
A pulse amidst the ebb and flow.

Fingers trace the cool, smooth pane,
Searching for a hand to hold.
In this world, love feels like pain,
As stories linger, yet untold.

Behind the glass, they dance alone,
Twilight whispers in the air.
Though surrounded, hearts feel like stone,
In this ballet, souls lay bare.

Translucent Echoes of Hope

In the stillness of dawn's embrace,
Whispers blend with morning light.
Colors shimmer, a gentle grace,
Painting soft dreams to take flight.

Each note rings in the open air,
A melody we yearn to find.
Resonance floats everywhere,
Carving paths in the mind, unblind.

Through the haze of doubt and fear,
Echoes carry tales of the brave.
In fragile voices, we draw near,
Claiming the hope we seek to save.

As shadows retreat with the day,
Translucent visions come alive.
Each echo sings in its own way,
In heartbeats, dreams revive.

Metamorphosis in Shadows

Beneath the cloak of midnight's shroud,
Life stirs quietly in the dark.
Twisted forms, once lost in crowd,
Begin to glow with hidden spark.

Silhouettes dance on the wall,
Stories writhe in twilight's breath.
Each wavering line stands tall,
Transforming fears and thoughts of death.

From ashes rise, new beings formed,
In the depths of darkest night.
Through their pain, bright hearts are warmed,
Emerging bold with gentle light.

Metamorphosis takes its time,
In shadows rich, the soul expands.
From despair, we forge the rhyme,
Crafting beauty with naked hands.

Gossamer Threads and Untold Stories

In whispers soft, the tales unfold,
Life's secrets woven, spun from gold.
Each fleeting moment, a fragile thread,
Binding our hearts, where dreams are led.

In laughter shared, and tears that flow,
Glimmers of truth in the ebb and glow.
Gossamer paths we wander and weave,
In the dance of life, believe, believe.

The stories linger, etched in time,
In each heartbeat, a rhythmic rhyme.
Fragments of light in the shadows cast,
Echoes of futures and memories past.

With open hearts, we paint the sky,
With colors of hope that never die.
Gossamer threads, with love entwined,
Charting the courses our souls have signed.

Shadows Cast by Fragile Hope

In the quiet dusk, where dreams reside,
Shadows whisper secrets, hearts confide.
Fragile hopes flicker like candles' flames,
Illuminating paths with unspoken names.

Each lingering shadow tells of despair,
Yet within the darkness, hope finds its air.
The softness of night, a gentle embrace,
Hiding the battles we bravely face.

With each passing moment, shadows grow long,
Yet the heart's quiet pulse remains strong.
In stillness we gather our strength anew,
The fragile hope guides us, steadfast and true.

Through trials we wander, with spirits aglow,
Emerging from shadows, we learn to grow.
For in every shadow, a beacon can shine,
Illuminating paths, where hope intertwines.

Wings Caught in Twilight's Grip

At twilight's edge, the world turns still,
Silent wings flutter, dreams fulfill.
Caught in the weave of the fading light,
A dance of shadows, a whispered flight.

The horizon glows with a dusky hue,
Promises linger in the shades of blue.
Wings stretching wide, yet tethered near,
In twilight's embrace, we conquer fear.

Soft murmurs of night, beckoning near,
In the hush of dusk, our dreams appear.
Yet, caught in the grip of day's farewell,
The heart's quiet longing begins to swell.

From dusk to dawn, the cycle spins,
Wings of the night carry soft violin.
In twilight's arms, we find our way,
Emerging from shadows, to greet the day.

Breaking Through Invisible Nets

In silence bound, like whispers confined,
Invisible nets, our dreams maligned.
But within the heart, a fire burns bright,
A longing for freedom, to take flight.

Each moment we gather, strength to defy,
To shatter the chains, let our spirits fly.
With courage as armor, we stand tall,
Breaking through barriers, we will not fall.

The nets may be woven with threads of doubt,
But we nurture hope that life's about.
With every heartbeat, we rise and break,
Invisible bonds, a chance to awake.

The dawn whispers softly, a new refrain,
From the ashes of setbacks, we rise again.
Breaking through darkness, we face the sun,
With hearts wide open, our journey's begun.

Fractals of the Unfurling Soul

In shadows deep, where whispers grow,
Patterns emerge, as rivers flow.
A mirror cracked, reflects the light,
Within the dark, dreams take flight.

Each breath a brushstroke on the night,
Colors blend in soft twilight.
A fractal maze, both wild and free,
Unlocking realms of mystery.

The heart expands, an ocean wide,
Waves of the past, in currents glide.
The tranquil pulse of ancient lore,
Guides the seeker to the shore.

Unfurling petals, secrets shade,
In every layer, stories laid.
Eternal spirals, rise and fall,
In fractals formed, we find it all.

Echoes of Rigid Horizons

Across the field, horizons bend,
Rigid lines that do not end.
Whispers of hope in chains confined,
Yet still, the heart seeks to unwind.

Mountains loom like sacred guards,
Shadows stretch and pull the shards.
In every crack, a melody,
Echoes press against the free.

Silent cries in windswept air,
Boundless dreams that dare to share.
The horizon's edge, a distant lie,
Truths emerge where eagles fly.

In the stillness, strength is found,
Roots that dig in solid ground.
Echoes call beyond the bars,
Rigid paths lead to the stars.

The Dance of Defiance and Delicacy

In twilight's glow, the dancers sway,
With lightness found in shades of gray.
A fierce resolve in gentle grace,
Each movement speaks of love's embrace.

Bold steps taken on fragile ground,
A story woven, profound sound.
Defiance born from softest heart,
In every twist, new worlds depart.

Veils of silk, spun with intent,
Every turn, a life well spent.
Resilience beckons, fierce and bright,
While delicate dreams take flight.

In harmony, the two align,
Delicate threads in strong design.
A dance between the dark and clear,
Infinitesimal, yet sincere.

Silken Threads and Frayed Ends

In the loom of life, threads are spun,
Each one tells tales of battles won.
Silken whispers of love and loss,
Binding hearts despite the cost.

Frayed edges speak of time's embrace,
Fragile beauty in every trace.
Woven patterns, chaos refined,
In the fabric, solace find.

The tapestry holds joy and pain,
In vibrant hues, and subtle stain.
Stories linger in every stitch,
Lives interwoven, none too rich.

Yet through the frays, new threads emerge,
From darkness springs a silent urge.
To weave anew from what we mend,
In silken threads, our lives extend.

Gilded Shadows of Twilight

In the dusk where dreams reside,
Whispers of the night abide.
Softly glow the fading light,
Gilded shadows take their flight.

Rippling echoes call my name,
Fleeting moments, brief but tame.
Nature wraps in velvet hues,
As the stars begin to fuse.

Crickets sing a lullaby,
Beneath the vast and starry sky.
Memories flicker, dance, and sway,
In the twilight's warm array.

Embers fade but love endures,
Through the night's enchanted tours.
In this realm where silence gleams,
Gilded shadows hold our dreams.

Unfolding in the Dim

In the corners cloaked in shade,
Hearts awaken, gently laid.
Silent moments, softly spun,
Unfolding threads, two become one.

Whispers brush against the skin,
Tales of longing tucked within.
Beneath the veil of muted light,
Hopes emerge, taking flight.

Time suspends in twilight's glow,
While the whispers start to flow.
Promises held in gentle hands,
Unraveled dreams like shifting sands.

In the dim, a dance begins,
Where the light and darkness spins.
Unfolding stories, pure and true,
In the shadows, me and you.

Through the Lattice of Yearning

Beyond the bars of time and fate,
Yearning whispers, don't wait.
Through the lattice, glimmers beam,
Framing every fragile dream.

Hopes that stretch beyond the night,
Searching for that distant light.
Each sigh a note, each wish a thread,
In the silence, love is fed.

Captured moments, fleeting grace,
Each heartbeat a warm embrace.
Through the lattice, shadows play,
In the longing, find our way.

Fingers trace the woven path,
Through the joy and through the wrath.
Yearning calls, we're drawn to sing,
Through the lattice, let love spring.

Captive Wishes Take Wing

Beneath the moon's soft, silver glow,
Captive wishes start to flow.
In the stillness, dreams take flight,
Carried forth into the night.

Each desire, a fragile spark,
Rising gently from the dark.
Wings of hope on tender streams,
Surfing currents crafted dreams.

Silent prayers and whispers bare,
Rising high on evening air.
With each flutter, hearts will cling,
To the magic we can bring.

As the dawn begins to break,
Captive wishes surely wake.
Set them free, let spirits sing,
In the light, our hopes take wing.

Celestial Visions

Stars whisper secrets bright,
In the stillness of the night.
Galaxies dance, twirl and spin,
Awakening dreams deep within.

Nebulae in colors bold,
Stories of the cosmos told.
Time unfurls in silent grace,
In the vastness, we find our place.

Comets streak with fiery tails,
Guiding us through cosmic trails.
In the heavens' endless sea,
We glimpse our shared eternity.

Earthbound Dreams

Beneath the boughs, shadows play,
Fleeting moments drift away.
Whispers of the earth so deep,
In their embrace, secrets keep.

Each petal holds a tale untold,
Of love and life, both brave and bold.
The breeze carries hopes on high,
As we watch the clouds drift by.

Mountains stand in silent pride,
Guardians of the dreams inside.
Rivers murmur soft and low,
In their currents, visions flow.

Unfurling Amidst Constraints

Within the walls, a flower grows,
Breaking free where sunlight flows.
Roots entwined in hardened soil,
Amidst the strife, the dreamers toil.

Against the weight, it seeks the light,
Reaching out with all its might.
Petals dance in gentle breeze,
A testament to nature's ease.

Like hearts confined, we stretch and strain,
In search of solace through the pain.
With every breath, we rise and shine,
In fragile forms, we intertwine.

The Garden's Silent Sentinels

In twilight's glow, the guardians stand,
Nurturing life with tender hand.
Flowers bloom, a vibrant display,
In their watchful presence, we sway.

Yet shadows linger, secrets keep,
In corners where the lost ones sleep.
Each leaf a whisper, soft and clear,
Nature's watch is always near.

Time pauses in this sacred space,
Protection felt in every trace.
The garden breathes, a living tome,
Within its depths, we find our home.

Cage of Color

Bars of hue bend the eye,
In a world where dreams can fly.
Prismed visions, vivid, bright,
Hold us captive in their light.

Yet within, the heart still beats,
Longing for the sun's warm sweeps.
Amidst the shades, wings flutter fast,
Hoping one day to break the cast.

Within this cage of vibrant strife,
We seek the edges of our life.
With courage born of sunlit rays,
We strive to carve our own pathways.

Caged in the Light of Day

Behind the bars, the sun does shine,
A world outside, so pure, divine.
But wings are clipped, the heart does ache,
Yearning for the chance to break.

Shadows dance upon the wall,
Echoes of a distant call.
Freedom whispers, soft and sweet,
Yet here I sit, bound in my seat.

Moments pass like drifting sand,
Hope flickers like a trembling hand.
In the light, I long to soar,
But fear keeps me at this door.

Yet in my heart, a spark ignites,
A dream unfolds in whispered nights.
With every breath, I stoke the flame,
To rise, to fly, to shed this name.

The Longing Within

Beneath the surface, a river flows,
In silence deep, the longing grows.
A whisper caught in the night air,
A flicker of hope, a distant prayer.

In every moment, shadows cast,
Reflections of a troubled past.
Yet in the stillness, truth reveals,
The depth of pain the heart distills.

Time slips through like grains of sand,
Each second lost, but I still stand.
For in this heart, a fire burns,
A chance for love, a world that turns.

Embracing dreams, I find my way,
Through darkest nights, into the day.
The longing fuels the path I tread,
With every step, the fears I shed.

Chains Painted in Color

Wrapped in hues of emerald green,
Chains that bind, yet still unseen.
Each link a story, a tale to tell,
Of battles fought, of dreams that fell.

Colors clash in vibrant strife,
Bound by choices, the weight of life.
Yet in this prison, art thrives bold,
A tapestry of hope retold.

Through the darkness, light may seep,
In shades so bright, the soul can leap.
Chains painted in colors bright and free,
Transforming pain to harmony.

With brush in hand, I find my voice,
Creating beauty from loss, a choice.
For though I'm bound, I still can sing,
Awakening the joy that dreams can bring.

A Symphony of Silent Flight

In the stillness, wings take form,
An unseen dance, a world reborn.
Notes of freedom, soft and clear,
Play the symphony we hold dear.

Through the quiet, echoes soar,
A melody of dreams once more.
In gentle whispers, secrets glide,
A tranquil journey, hearts collide.

Above the clouds, beyond the fray,
Silent flights on silver rays.
A symphony of hope unfurls,
In the heart of all our worlds.

Together in this boundless space,
We find our rhythm, our own grace.
In every heart, the song ignites,
A symphony of silent flights.

Beyond the Hurdles of Transformation

Each step we take, a mile to go,
The weight of doubt begins to grow.
Yet through the trials, we stand tall,
For every stumble, we can recall.

Shadows of fear may cast their gloom,
But deep within, we find the bloom.
With courage found in each refrain,
We learn to dance through joy and pain.

Metamorphosis, a constant fight,
Emerging strong into the light.
The hurdles now, a past constraint,
With wings of hope, we rise, we paint.

Beyond the hurdles, we embrace,
A world anew, a boundless space.
With every breath, we boldly strive,
In transformation, we come alive.

The Lattice of Unexplored Skies

A tapestry of stars unfolds,
In quiet whispers, mysteries told.
The shimmering paths, both near and far,
Guide our hearts like a northern star.

Winds of change, they softly call,
To venture forth, to rise, to fall.
Every breath, a chance to soar,
With open hearts, we crave for more.

Mountains stand, yet spirits fly,
Across the lattice of the sky.
Where dreams are stitched with threads of light,
And every shadow births the night.

Unexplored realms await our gaze,
In splendid hues, the world ablaze.
Together we will chart the map,
In unity, we close the gap.

An Elegy to the Unwinged

In silence, they tread upon the ground,
With heavy hearts, their hopes are drowned.
Yet even roots, they whisper dreams,
Of soaring high through sunlit beams.

An elegy rests upon the breeze,
For those who long for lifted trees.
Their spirits yearn for skies above,
A lament sung for the unwinged love.

Yet in their eyes, the stars reside,
A glimmer bright, they cannot hide.
In shadows deep, their stories bloom,
A testament within the gloom.

So let us sing of dreams unchained,
For every heart that has remained.
In unity, we find our way,
With wings unseen, we still can play.

Embracing the Edge of Flight

On precipices, we find our fate,
Where courage and longing gently wait.
With arms outstretched, we greet the sky,
In moments fierce, we learn to fly.

The edge may tremble, fears ignite,
Yet in the heart, there's fierce delight.
With every leap, our spirits rise,
Embracing dreams that touch the skies.

In vast horizons, dreams take form,
We shape our world through every storm.
Together, we will leap and glide,
In freedom's dance, our souls abide.

So here we stand, on wings of grace,
Embracing life, we find our place.
With every beat, our hearts align,
At the edge of flight, our spirits shine.

Whispers of the Winged Soul

In quiet shadows, dreams take flight,
Softly weaving through the night.
Echoed whispers, tales untold,
A journey woven, brave and bold.

Wings unfurl, embraced by air,
Glimmers of hope, beyond despair.
Stars align in the silent sweep,
The secrets of the heart we keep.

Through gentle breezes, thoughts will sway,
In the realm where spirits play.
Invisible paths, we follow true,
Awakening worlds anew.

As dawn awakens the slumbering sky,
The winged soul learns to fly.
With every whisper, love calls near,
In the heart's chamber, free from fear.

Enclosed in a Kaleidoscope

Colors dance in a ceaseless swirl,
Fragments of light in a vibrant whirl.
Patterns shift, reshape the view,
Each moment crafted, fresh and new.

Through prisms bright, the visions flow,
Enchanted scenes that gently glow.
Textures merge in a rhythm divine,
In this maze, our spirits twine.

Laughter rings, like chimes in the air,
Echoing joy everywhere.
Hearts aligned, a tapestry seams,
Woven together in shared dreams.

As shades blend in rich delight,
The kaleidoscope spins through the night.
Holding wonders, forever embraced,
In this journey, we are traced.

The Tug of Invisible Threads

Tied to memories, unseen yet strong,
Threads of fate, weaves our song.
With every heartbeat, we connect,
In life's fabric, souls reflect.

A gentle pull, it leads us near,
Bound together, year by year.
Through joy and sorrow, the fibers tug,
An endless bond, a loving hug.

In moments shared, the ties grow tight,
As stars align, igniting light.
Lifetimes woven, in laughter and tears,
A tapestry rich through all our years.

Each thread a story waiting to blend,
With every stitch, together we mend.
And though unseen, this love remains,
A dance of souls through joy and pains.

Restrained Elegance

In whispers soft, a grace concealed,
A beauty held, yet never revealed.
Lines that curve with silent intent,
In quietude, their glory spent.

With every gesture, poised and calm,
A hint of strength, like nature's balm.
Draped in shadows, a delicate art,
A ballet spun from the heart.

Threads of gold in a tapestry spun,
Defining lines where dreams have begun.
Fleeting glimpses, a graceful tease,
In every pause, our souls find peace.

Restrained yet radiant, the spirit flows,
Like petals whispering in the rose.
In stillness found, a world unfolds,
Elegance wrapped in timeless holds.

The Art of Limitation's Grace

In narrow paths, we find our way,
A canvas small, our colors play.
Each choice we make, a gentle sigh,
Within the bounds, our spirits fly.

The beauty lies in what we hold,
In whispers soft, in stories told.
With every limit, a chance to see,
The art of grace in simplicity.

We shape our world with careful hands,
In simple truths, our heart understands.
As shadows dance on fleeting light,
We craft our dreams through day and night.

So let us cherish what we trust,
In every moment, find the just.
For in limitation, we will find,
The grace that frees the heart and mind.

Horizon's Edge and Golden Fringes

The waking sun paints skies so bright,
A fleeting dream in morning light.
To chase the edge where worlds align,
Where golden fringes weave and shine.

At horizon's edge, we stand in awe,
With endless tales and sights to draw.
Each step we take, a journey's thread,
To lands where hopes and wishes spread.

The painted sky, a canvas wide,
Where secrets hide and dreams abide.
In every hue, a promise lingers,
The beauty found in golden fingers.

As daylight fades, the stars awake,
A tapestry that fate can make.
With every glance at twilight's glow,
The horizon beckons, we shall go.

Dreams Entangled in Still Air

In stillness deep, our dreams take flight,
Carried softly on the night.
Entangled hopes in whispered prayer,
A dance of thoughts in gentle air.

With every breath, a story spun,
In woven dreams 'til night is done.
The stillness wraps around us tight,
Beneath the stars, the world feels right.

Echoes linger, fading slow,
As dawn approaches, dreams must go.
Yet in the hush, we plant the seed,
Of all the dreams that gently lead.

So let us cherish moments small,
In still air's embrace, we stand tall.
In dreams entangled, we remain,
For in that stillness, love's refrain.

Ephemeral Routes We Never Took

Along the path where shadows play,
Lie routes unchosen every day.
Each turn we missed, a door ajar,
In dreams of journeys near and far.

The road less traveled calls our name,
With whispers sweet of distant fame.
Yet here we stand, at fate's own gate,
In paths undone, we contemplate.

Through fleeting moments, time does flash,
In choices made, in dreams we clash.
What might have been, a haunting song,
In ephemeral trails, we belong.

Though routes may fade like morning dew,
In every choice, a hint of blue.
For in our hearts, those routes will stay,
A map of dreams that light the way.

Threads of an Unwoven Sky

In the tapestry of twilight,
Stars weave dreams so bright,
Each thread a whispered wish,
Lost in the silent night.

Clouds drift like wayward thoughts,
Painting tales on the breeze,
A canvas of fleeting time,
Unbound by reality's keys.

Colors swirl in gentle dance,
As shadows softly play,
In twilight's gentle grasp,
The night claims the day.

Yet in this fragile moment,
Hope twinkling from afar,
Threads of an unwoven sky,
Guide us to who we are.

Flights of Fancy

Upon the wings of daydreams,
We rise above the mundane,
Where impossible tales birth,
In every heartbeat's refrain.

Through fields of golden wishes,
We dance among the stars,
Every glance a new adventure,
Every laugh leaves no scars.

Clouds become our pillows,
As we drift through endless skies,
In the realm of pure imagination,
Where freedom never dies.

So let us chase horizons,
Embrace the magic we find,
For in these flights of fancy,
Our hearts are intertwined.

Grounded Reality

In the quiet of the morning,
Life awakens anew,
With every ray of sunshine,
A promise starts to brew.

Roots sink deep in earth's embrace,
Holding dreams firm and fast,
In the garden of our choices,
We cultivate our past.

Every step upon this soil,
Echoes of those who came,
Their hopes and burdens linger,
In the whispers of their names.

Yet amidst the winds of change,
We find a strength to stand,
In grounded reality,
Together, hand in hand.

The Cloak of Enchantment

Beneath a canopy of stars,
Magic weaves its spell,
Each moment filled with wonder,
In the shadows where we dwell.

A cloak spun from dreams so bright,
Enfolds us in its grace,
We dance upon the starlit paths,
In this enchanted space.

Every sigh, a tender secret,
Every heartbeat, a song,
We twirl in the moonlight's glow,
Where we both belong.

So let us wear this mystery,
Embrace what lies ahead,
For in the cloak of enchantment,
All fears and doubts are shed.

Surrendered to the Winds of Fate

Like leaves that drift in autumn's breath,
We float on currents bold,
Surrendered to the whims of fate,
Stories waiting to be told.

Through valleys low and mountains high,
We journey without fear,
Embracing every twist and turn,
As fate guides us near.

In the dance of chance and fortune,
Life's tapestry we weave,
With every choice a pathway forged,
In what we dare believe.

So let us trust the winds that blow,
And follow where they lead,
For in surrender lies the strength,
To fulfill our heart's deep need.

Wings of Fractured Freedom

In shadows cast by restless sighs,
Hope lingers where the spirit flies.
Yet chains of doubt hold tightly fast,
Each whispered dream, a ghost from past.

The sky above, a realm of light,
Calls out to souls who crave the flight.
With every beat of fractured wing,
The heart awakens, begins to sing.

Beneath the weight of silent cries,
Visions bloom where courage lies.
In broken nights, the stars align,
To guide the lost through space and time.

Together we'll reconstruct the dawn,
From shards of night, a new hymn drawn.
From every fall, we rise anew,
With wings of hope, we'll pierce the blue.

Chasing Colors in the Wind

A canvas painted with the breeze,
Vivid hues that swirl and tease.
Each whisper brings a laugh, a spark,
In the tapestry of light and dark.

Through meadows lush and valleys wide,
We dance where wildflowers abide.
The wind, a brush that sweeps the air,
Sketches moments that we both share.

Chasing colors, hearts entwined,
In every shade, a story signed.
The world flares bright, then fades away,
Yet in this chase, our spirits stay.

Lost in the rhythm, free and bold,
A vibrant tale yet to be told.
With every gust, our laughter spins,
Chasing colors, where love begins.

Cocooned Dreams and Hidden Paths

In silence wrapped, the dreams are spun,
In tender threads, the stories run.
Cocooned in hope, they softly gleam,
Awaiting dawn to break the dream.

Each hidden path, a beckoning light,
Whispers beckon through the night.
With every step, the heart ignites,
To chase the shadows, seek new heights.

The journey's long, but brightly paved,
With courage strong, the fears are braved.
Through twisted woods and streams unseen,
We find the realms where we have been.

Cocooned dreams unfold in time,
Revealing truths in whispered rhyme.
From hidden paths, our souls break free,
To dance in light, eternally.

The Flight of Silent Echoes

In empty halls where whispers dwell,
The echoes float, a ghostly spell.
Each silent flight, a fleeting trace,
Of moments lost, yet full of grace.

Through twilight hues and shadows long,
The heart remembers every song.
In stillness reigns a trembling peace,
Where echoes linger, never cease.

With open arms, the night enfolds,
Unraveling secrets never told.
In every sigh, a memory clear,
The flight of echoes pulling near.

A gentle breeze, a soft goodbye,
In whispered tones, our spirits fly.
Across the void, a bridge we find,
In silent echoes, love unlined.

Tethered Dreams

In twilight's glow, the whispers play,
A dance of wishes, lost and stray.
Beneath the stars, our hopes take flight,
Yet tethered dreams cling tight to night.

Through silver mist, they softly roam,
In pages worn, they seek a home.
But shadows linger, doubts increase,
As every heartbeat calls for peace.

With every dawn, the light unfurls,
A tapestry of hidden pearls.
Yet still we chase the fleeting breeze,
As tethered dreams bring us to our knees.

So linger here, where visions weave,
In silent thoughts, we must believe.
We'll find our strength, reclaim the theme,
And rise anew from tethered dreams.

Gilded Pain

In golden chains, sweet sorrow clings,
A heavy heart that softly sings.
Each note a tear, each sigh a plea,
Gilded pain, it seeks to be free.

The echoes ring in hollow halls,
Where laughter lingers, memory calls.
Yet every joy is laced with strife,
A tapestry of grief and life.

With every scar, a tale is spun,
Of battles lost, and victories won.
Through every wound, the light remains,
In every heart, the gilded pain.

So let us dance in shadows deep,
Embrace the hurt, for it will keep.
In gilded hues, we paint our fate,
In every tear, we find our state.

The Veil of Unfulfilled Journeys

Behind the veil, the shadows sigh,
Of journeys long, that time let die.
In whispers soft, they call our name,
Yet fade away, like fleeting flame.

Through winding paths, our footsteps trace,
The dreams deferred, a ghostly space.
With heavy hearts, we search the night,
For unfulfilled journeys that feel right.

But hope still glimmers, faint yet true,
In every star that pierces blue.
The veil may dim, but won't obscure,
The longing hearts that still endure.

So lift the veil, and set your sights,
On distant shores and shining lights.
For every journey, though it bends,
May lead us back to where it ends.

Songs of the Boundless Heart

In every heartbeat, music swells,
A symphony where beauty dwells.
With every breath, a song takes flight,
Of boundless love that fills the night.

With tender notes, the spirit soars,
Beyond the walls, through open doors.
In every glance, the cosmos hums,
A melody that ever drums.

Through storms and calm, the voices rise,
In unison beneath the skies.
The boundless heart, it knows no end,
In every tune, our souls transcend.

So let us sing, in joy and pain,
In every loss, we still shall gain.
For in the songs of hearts alive,
The boundless spirit learns to thrive.

Dappled Shadows over Stifled Flight

In dappled light, the shadows play,
Where dreams are trapped, and hopes decay.
Stifled flight beneath the trees,
A silent whisper in the breeze.

With every branch, the stories weave,
Of longing souls that yearn to leave.
Yet in the shade, they find their place,
In dappled shadows, a soft embrace.

With every flutter, wings are bound,
In quiet corners, solace found.
Though stifled, yet they learn to glow,
In dappled shadows, hearts still flow.

So let the sun break through the night,
To free the souls and grant them flight.
In every shadow, dreams delight,
And find their way through stifled flight.

Petals of Gold in an Iron Grip

In a garden where dreams unfold,
Petals shimmer, glistening bold.
Iron bars, a watchful eye,
Hold the beauty, yet it sighs.

Through cracked concrete, hope does seep,
Whispers of secrets, shadows keep.
In this prison, life still dares,
Each golden petal, love declares.

The sunbreaks through, a tender beam,
Chasing away the darkest dream.
With every breeze, a soft caress,
In the grip, there's still finesse.

Petals bend, but never break,
In the shadows, they still wake.
Holding on to what they know,
Even trapped, they find their glow.

The Dance of the Unseen

In twilight's grasp, the whispers play,
Shadows twirl in a ghostly sway.
Mountains echo the silent song,
Where echoes of the lost belong.

Beneath the moon's watchful sheen,
Figures glide, elusive, keen.
In silence, hearts begin to weave,
A symphony that time won't leave.

With every step, a tale untold,
In the dark, they twist and fold.
The dance of dreams, a fleeting chance,
Life's secrets hidden in each glance.

They twine in patterns, bold yet slight,
Dancing shadows claim the night.
Unseen beauty finds its way,
In the dusk, where spirits play.

Colors of Imprisoned Whimsy

Beneath the sky, a canvas rare,
Colors burst, but none to share.
Each hue locked in a heart's embrace,
Imprisoned dreams seek to find space.

Brushstrokes of laughter, shades of tears,
Whimsy held by chains of fears.
In the gray, a flicker bold,
Stories of joy yet to be told.

A palette yearning for release,
Each color dreams of sweet caprice.
To dance in daylight's warm sigh,
Where every shade can learn to fly.

Behind the bars of muted tones,
Life awaits, as spirit groans.
Colors clash, but hope shines true,
Imprisoned whimsy breaks anew.

Shadows of the Unexplored

In the depths where silence reigns,
Shadows weave like phantom chains.
Here the unknown softly stirs,
Whispers carried on the blurs.

Uncharted paths, a beckoning call,
Where secrets lurk, awaiting all.
Every corner, a story waits,
In the dark, a heart elates.

Footsteps echo on ancient ground,
Unseen wonders stir around.
A flicker sparks, ignites the mind,
In shadows, treasures we may find.

With courage stitched in every seam,
We tread the borders of the dream.
In whispers soft, the wild implores,
To dance with shadows, unlock the doors.

Invisible Borders of the Soul

Within the heart, a silent wall,
Unseen edges, where shadows fall.
Whispers echo, dreams take flight,
Crossing realms, hidden from sight.

Companions bound by silent ties,
Beneath the moon, where truth defies.
In the quiet, secrets weave,
Invisible borders, we believe.

Each tear a river, each laugh a bridge,
Connecting worlds, we dare to ridge.
In depth and silence, hearts collide,
A tapestry unspooled, side by side.

Yet through these walls, a light can seep,
Through cracks of pain, a promise keeps.
With every breath, we break the mold,
Invisible borders, stories told.

Tethered to Earth

Roots delve deep in the soil's embrace,
Anchoring dreams in a steadfast place.
With every breeze, whispers of home,
Tethered to earth, where our spirits roam.

In the embrace of the ancient trees,
Stories linger in the rustling leaves.
Grounded in love, yet longing to fly,
Tethered to earth, we still reach for sky.

Each step we take on this well-worn ground,
In the dance of life, our pulses sound.
From whispers to shouts, we plant our seeds,
Tethered to earth, fulfilling our needs.

Yet in the dusk, when shadows bloom,
We dream of heights, escaping the gloom.
With hearts so brave, we'll chase the stars,
Tethered to earth, yet free in our scars.

Yearning for Sky

In twilight's glow, we lift our gaze,
Yearning for sky, through dusky haze.
Clouds of hope drift softly by,
Whispers of dreams, we won't deny.

In endless blue, our spirits soar,
Seeking the heavens, forevermore.
Each heartbeat loud, like thunder's call,
Yearning for sky, we rise or fall.

Beneath the weight of earthly bind,
We chase the light, leaving fears behind.
In the vast expanse, we dare to roam,
Yearning for sky, we find our home.

Yet in the silence, our souls take flight,
Embracing stars, igniting the night.
Through every tear, we learn to fly,
In the sacred quest, yearning for sky.

Chained by the Colors We Wear

In garments bright, our stories hide,
Chained by colors, the masks we bide.
In vibrant hues, our souls entrapped,
A canvas painted, feelings wrapped.

Each shade a whisper, a tale to tell,
Of joy and sorrow, of heaven and hell.
Yet beneath the layers, hearts beat bare,
Chained by colors, but longing to share.

In shades of grey, we find our truth,
Worn with pride, a sign of youth.
In every stitch, a woven prayer,
Chained by colors, we breathe the air.

To break the chains, a quest we choose,
To unveil the essence, to lose the ruse.
In colors bold, we stand and dare,
Chained by colors, yet free in the air.

Echoes of a Furling Wing

In the hush of dawn, a whisper grows,
Echoes of a furling wing, it flows.
Through silent skies, the shadows dance,
Carried on breeze, in fate's expanse.

With every flight, memories unfurl,
Tracing the arcs of a fleeting swirl.
In radiant hues, the moments cling,
Echoes of a furling wing, they sing.

Through valleys deep, and mountains high,
We chase the echoes, we learn to fly.
In the soft caress, we find our spring,
Echoes of a furling wing, take wing.

As day meets night, in twilight's seam,
We weave the threads of a vivid dream.
With every pulse, the heart's string sings,
In the stillness, echoes of a furling wing.

Threads of Dusk

In twilight's embrace, the shadows weave,
Soft whispers of night, as day takes leave.
Stars slowly blink in the deepening sky,
Where dreams intertwine, as moments pass by.

A tapestry spun from the golden glow,
Each thread a memory, in twilight's flow.
Colors fade gently, dusk's gentle sigh,
Painting the world where the soft shadows lie.

Silhouettes dance on the edge of the light,
As echoes of laughter fade into night.
The horizon blushes with secrets untold,
In threads of dusk, a story unfolds.

Underneath stars, when silence takes flight,
We find in the dusk the beauty of night.
Life's fleeting moments, a delicate trust,
Woven together in threads of dusk's rust.

Paths of Dawn

Morning breaks gently, a whispering glow,
Awakening dreams that lingered below.
Sunshine spills over the hills like a stream,
Casting a light, igniting a dream.

Fingers of light stretch across muted plains,
Chasing the shadows, dissolving the chains.
Birds serenade with a song crystal clear,
Inviting our hearts to welcome the year.

Each step we take on this path of new day,
Illuminates choices in a brilliant array.
Life unfolds sweetly, each moment a gift,
On paths of dawn, our spirits can lift.

As colors burst forth in the soft morning air,
Hope dances lightly, beyond all despair.
From darkness to light, a journey divine,
On paths of dawn, where our dreams intertwine.

Masks of Flight in Stillness

In quiet corners where secrets reside,
The masks we wear, they softly collide.
Like birds in pause, in the stillness we find,
A dance in the silence, a flight intertwined.

The heart beats softly, a rhythm concealed,\nIn the calm
of the moment, our truths are revealed.
We drift on whispers, our spirits take wing,
In shadows of silence, we learn how to sing.

With every heartbeat, the lies fall away,
Unveiling the dreams that our souls long to play.
In the stillness, we lift, break free from the night,
Embracing the freedom, the masks take their flight.

A tapestry woven from hopes tightly held,
In stillness, our spirit's true colors are spelled.
So let us surrender to the gentle embrace,
Where masks of flight find their rightful place.

Hues of Hope

Colors unfurl in the warmth of the day,
Each hue a promise, come what may.
In laughter and tears, they blend and they shine,
A palette of dreams that are yours and mine.

Crimson for passion, the fire of the heart,
Emerald for growth, where new journeys start.
Golden horizons that stretch to the sky,
Remind us of moments that gently pass by.

With every sunrise, the canvas renews,
A spectrum of feelings, a mix of our views.
Pastels of kindness, rich indigo grace,
In hues of hope, we find our true place.

So let us paint boldly, with strokes strong and true,
In the gallery of life, each shade's made for you.
With colors that dance, we'll forever cope,
Creating a masterpiece filled with our hope.

Shadows of the Past

In echoes of whispers, the shadows emerge,
Memories linger, like waves in a surge.
Faded photographs, a canvas of time,
Each moment a heartbeat, a rhythm, a rhyme.

Through corridors where silence tends to creep,
The past holds its secrets, it's ours to keep.
In twilight reflections, we face what we've lost,
Embracing the lessons, regardless of cost.

The paths we have traveled, though rugged and steep,
Have forged who we are in the truth we now reap.
Carried by time, the shadows still dance,
In the light of forgiveness, we give it a chance.

So let us not dwell on the pain that has passed,
But honor the journey, our shadows amassed.
With wisdom we've gained, and strength from the last,
We greet every dawn, leaving shadows in cast.

The Garden of Longing

In a secret garden where wishes bloom wide,
A tapestry woven with dreams deep inside.
Petals of yearning, the fragrance of hope,
In the beauty of longing, our spirits elope.

Nurtured by patience, the blossoms take root,
With each gentle sigh, a new journey's pursuit.
The weeping willows, they cradle our dreams,
As sunlight cascades through delicate beams.

Embrace the silence, the whispers of night,
In the garden of longing, our hearts find their light.
Each flower a story, each leaf a sweet song,
In the richness of yearning, we find where we belong.

So wander with wisdom through this sacred place,
The garden awaits with a warm, loving grace.
In the depth of desire, we nurture and tend,
In the garden of longing, our spirits transcend.

Milton Keynes UK
Ingram Content Group UK Ltd.
UKHW022223251124
451566UK00006B/96